Samantha Smith:

The Girl Who Dreamed of Peace

By Tracy Lynn Meyers

This book is dedicated to the memory of Samantha Smith and her dream of world peace, and to Arthur Smith, her beloved father.

Samantha Reed Smith: June 29, 1972- August 25, 1985

Cyrus Arthur Smith: August 12, 1940- August 25, 1985

If you are interested in publishing this book or would like to contact the author, write to:

Tracy Lynn Meyers
PO Box 1523
Oakdale, CA 95361

The photographs contained in this book are courtesy of The Samantha Smith Foundation (www.samanthasmith.info). All rights are retained by their original owners.

MEET SAMANTHA SMITH

Ten-year-old Samantha Smith rarely thought about politics. A typical fifth grader from Manchester, Maine with long brown hair, big blue eyes, and a dimpled grin, Samantha was always up for doing something fun. She was an active girl who loved playing softball, riding her bike, romping around with her dog Kim, and hanging out with her best friend Lynn. She enjoyed reading and liked science, but struggled with math. Samantha hoped to one day become a veterinarian. Her friendly nature and cheerful personality made her well-liked by other children, adults, and the animals she adored. Samantha's father Arthur was an English professor who taught writing and literature at the University of Maine in Augusta, and her mother Jane was employed as a social worker for the Maine State Department of Human Services. The Smiths considered themselves a normal family, and never dreamed that one day their only child would become a famous international figure and promoter of world peace. But, as Samantha later explained, everything changed once she began to worry that there might be a war.

THE LETTER

On Tuesday, April 12th, 1983, Samantha Smith, a fifth grade student at Manchester Elementary School, was suddenly called to the principal's office. Samantha was a little bit worried, but couldn't think of any reason why she might be in trouble. Samantha was a fun-loving girl, but she was also well behaved, and she couldn't recall doing anything wrong. When she reached the front office, Samantha was relieved to find out that there was not an upset principal, but rather an unexpected phone call, waiting for her. The school secretary, Mrs. Peabody, informed Samantha that a news reporter had called and was waiting to speak with her. Samantha insisted that that there must be some mistake. Mrs. Peabody replied, "Well, did you write a letter or something to Yuri Andropov?" The secretary pulled a surprised Samantha towards a chair, where she sat down and took the telephone. On the other end of the line was a reporter from a news agency called United Press International that distributed articles and photographs to newspaper, radio, and television stations all over the world. The eager reporter asked if she was indeed Samantha Smith, and if it was true that she had recently written a letter to Soviet leader Yuri Andropov. Samantha said yes, and was amazed to learn that parts of her letter had just been published halfway around the globe! The day before, a communist newspaper named *Pravda* had printed excerpts of several letters written by American citizens to the newly appointed Andropov. One of the letters quoted in the article was that of young Samantha Smith, who had asked Mr. Andropov, "Why do you want to conquer the whole world, or at least our country?" and begged to know if he was "going to vote to have a war or not?" *Pravda* seemed to find Samantha's questions amusing, and considered her ideas to be those of a naïve child. However, they felt that Samantha could be forgiven for her misconceptions due to the fact that she was only ten years old. Samantha wasn't discouraged by *Pravda* making her sound like a silly little schoolgirl, or even her classmates' lack of interest when she told them about her letter. When Samantha returned home from school that same day, she  immediately wrote another letter, this time to the Soviet Embassy in Washington, D.C., asking if Andropov was going to answer her questions, because they were good ones and it shouldn't matter that she was only ten years old. About a week later, Samantha got yet another surprise phone call. A Soviet ambassador informed Samantha that a letter from Andropov, written in English, was on its way, and that she should be getting it soon. Samantha joked that the man on the phone with the heavy accent sounded like someone out of a movie, and at first she thought that it might be one of her father's friends playing a joke on her. But true to his word, a few days later the Manchester post office phoned the Smith residence to say that a registered letter in a peculiar envelope had arrived for Samantha. On April 25th, Samantha and her father made a stop on her way to school to pick up the letter from Yuri Andropov that was awaiting her at the post office. Samantha was running late and barely had time to skim over the two-and-a-half page letter before arriving at Manchester Elementary. It read:

Dear Samantha,

I received your letter, which is like many others that have reached me from your country and from other countries around the world.

It seems to me-I can tell by your letter- that you are a courageous and honest girl, resembling Becky, the friend of Tom Sawyer in the famous book of your compatriot Mark Twain. This book is well known and loved in our country by all boys and girls.

You write that you are anxious about whether there will be a nuclear war between our two countries. And you ask are we doing anything so that war will not break out.

Your question is the most important of those that every thinking man can pose. I will reply to you seriously and honestly.

Yes, Samantha, we in the Soviet Union are trying to do everything so that there will not be war between our countries, so that in general there will not be war on earth. This is what every Soviet man wants. This is what the great founder of our state, Vladimir Lenin, taught us.
Soviet people well know what a terrible thing war is. Forty-two years ago, Nazi Germany, which strived for supremacy over the whole world, attacked our country, burned and destroyed many thousands of our towns and villages, killed millions of Soviet men, women, and children.

In that war, which ended with our victory, we were in alliance with the United States; together we fought for the liberation of many people from the Nazi invaders. I hope that you know about this from your history lessons in school. And today we want very much to live in peace, to trade and cooperate with all our neighbors on this earth- with those far way and those near by. And certainly with such a great country as the United States of America.

In America and in our country there are nuclear weapons- terrible weapons that can kill millions of people in an instant. But we do not want them to ever be used. That's precisely why the Soviet Union solemnly declared throughout the entire world that never-never-will it use nuclear weapons first against any country. In general we propose to discontinue further production of them and to proceed to the abolition of all the stockpiles on earth.

It seems to me that this is a sufficient answer to your second question: "Why do you want to wage war against the whole world or at least the United States?" We want nothing of the kind. No one in our country- neither workers, peasants, writers, nor doctors, neither grown-ups nor children, nor members of the government- want either a big or a "little" war.

We want peace- there is something that we are occupied with: growing wheat, building and inventing, writing books and flying into space. We want peace for ourselves and for all peoples of the planet. For our children and for you, Samantha.

I invite you, if your parents will let you, to come to our country, the best time being this summer. You will find out about our country, meet with your contemporaries, visit an international children's camp-"Artek"- on the sea. And see for yourself: in the Soviet Union, everyone is for peace and friendship among peoples.

Thank you for your letter. I wish you all the best in your young life.

Y. Andropov

Samantha asked her father if they could really accept Andropov's invitation and go to the Soviet Union. He answered, "We'll see," which is what he always said before saying yes! Samantha "just knew they would be going to Russia." (Samantha later read that Russia should actually be called the Soviet Union, and the people living there should be called Soviets, because although Russia is the largest republic in the Soviet Union and most Soviets have Russian heritage and speak the Russian language, there *are* some parts of the country that are not Russian.) After school that afternoon, Samantha looked forward to seeing her faithful dog Kim waiting to greet her as usual when she got off the bus. Instead, Samantha found her front yard full of reporters and cameramen who were taking her picture and asking her questions. Samantha was shocked and surprised by the sudden flood of attention. She repeatedly showed her letter from Andropov to the curious reporters who requested to see it, some of whom were

invited into the Smiths' bright and sunny kitchen. Samantha sat down at a table and told the press that she thought the letter from Andropov sounded as though it was "from a friend," and that Andropov seemed to have a sense of humor, which she hadn't expected. For the remainder of the day, the Smith's yellow telephone was ringing off the hook. Samantha's father even had to stay home from work to answer the phone, which rang "about every two minutes all day long." Soon, news crews from other countries such as France started showing up at Samantha's house, as well. Samantha thought it was comical when a Soviet journalist interviewed *her*, and then an American journalist interviewed *him*! Samantha also found it bizarre that the news people kept asking her the same questions over and over. "I asked them, why can't you ask me a question, and then pass around the answers? I mean… Here it costs a fortune to come talk to me, when they could simply get it from another reporter." In one telephone interview, Samantha explained that she first got the idea of writing to Andropov from her mother. "There was always something on television about missiles and nuclear bombs," Samantha recalled. She knew that nuclear bombs were dangerous weapons that could destroy the earth and its atmosphere. She was further aware of how the United States and the Soviet Union, the country also referred to as Russia, were in the middle of a "cold war." Although no actual fighting had broken out between the two great nations, the United States and the Soviet Union were considered enemies, and both were building more and more bombs in case an actual war was to start. The American and Soviet governments had very different opinions about how to run their countries. While the United States was- and still is- built on freedom and democracy, the Soviet Union believed in communism, wherein the government owned and controlled almost everything, including education, transportation, communication, farms, and factories. These political differences were causing fear and tension between the opposing countries. Samantha asked her mother if there was going to be a war. "I woke up one morning and wondered if this was going to be the last day of the Earth," Samantha remembered. "I asked my mother who would start a war and why." In an effort to ease Samantha's mind and try to explain why these bad feelings existed between the United States and the Soviet Union, Jane Smith sat down with her daughter and read to her about relations between the two powerful countries. Yet,

Samantha was still confused. She didn't understand why they would start a war that nobody could win, and that neither side wanted. Samantha suggested that her mother write a letter to Andropov and ask him this important question, but her mother replied, "Why don't you?" So in November of 1982, Samantha decided to compose a letter to the Soviet leader. "I just wanted to know what Andropov was like," Samantha later explained, adding, "If you get a letter back from someone, you get to know what he's like." Samantha admitted, however, that she "didn't think anything would happen" because of her letter. Nevertheless, Samantha did not use her typewriter but instead chose to hand write a one page letter to Andropov expressing her fears about the possibility of a nuclear war between their countries. Samantha joked that because her penmanship wasn't always very neat, she'd used her most "careful handwriting" so that Andropov wouldn't have any trouble reading her letter, which said:

Dear Mr. Andropov,

My name is Samantha Smith. I am ten years old. Congratulations on your new job. I have been worrying about Russia and the United States getting into a nuclear war. Are you going to vote to have a war or not? I you aren't please tell me how you are going to help to not have a war. This question you do not have to answer, but I would like to know why you want to conquer the world or at least our country. God made the world for us to live together in peace and not to fight.

Sincerely,
Samantha Smith

Samantha asked her parents to read the letter and make sure that she hadn't said anything wrong. Samantha certainly did not want to offend the Soviet world leader! Afterwards, not knowing the exact address to use, Samantha simply addressed her letter to "Yuri Andropov, the Kremlin, Moscow, U.S.S.R.," pasted two stamps on the envelope, and gave it to her father to mail. "It was a nice letter," commented Arthur Smith, noting, "She has always been a good writer." This wasn't the first time that Samantha had reached out and written to a famous politician. At the age of 5,  Samantha penned a letter to Queen Elizabeth of England, and had gotten a response from one of her ladies-in-waiting. After hearing from Andropov, Samantha considered writing more letters to both Princess Diana of Wales and President of the United States Ronald Reagan.

MEDIA FRENZY

After portions of Samantha's letter were printed in *Pravda* and news of her response from Andropov spread, the Associated Press sent a reporter to Manchester and took a photo of a grinning Samantha sitting in front of her father's typewriter. *People* magazine arrived shortly thereafter and published pictures of the Smith family posing on the back steps of their home.

"This is just proof that letter writing works and people do pay attention," Arthur declared. Within days, not only newspaper and magazine reporters, but also television producers, were requesting interviews with Samantha, who traveled across the country and appeared on such popular programs as *The Today Show* in  New York, where she got to see famous sites like the Statue of Liberty and the Bronx Zoo before attending a Broadway play, and *The Tonight Show* in California, where, according to Samantha, everyone shook your hand and kissed you. Unfortunately, no one in the town of Manchester got to witness Samantha being interviewed by Johnny Carson on national television, because instead of airing *The Tonight Show* as scheduled, the local tv station showed a Boston Red Socks baseball game instead! Luckily, Samantha received a copy of her talk show appearance on videotape, and the first time Samantha actually saw herself on television, she got tears in her eyes. On the other hand, Samantha found it funny when she was given articles about herself that she couldn't even read because they were written in foreign languages! Shortly after a single letter gained Samantha almost instant fame, Arthur warned his daughter not to let all of the attention go to her head, because it would "only last for a few days." Obviously, the Smiths had no clue of just how monumental this particular letter would become, and where it would lead them! Yet, despite being in the spotlight, young Samantha remained the same down-to-earth girl she'd always been, (even amusing one reporter by answering the door wearing roller skates!) and one month after receiving a reply to her letter, the Smith family decided that Samantha could accept Andropov's invitation to visit the Soviet Union. At first, Samantha's parents weren't sure if the trip was such a good idea for their daughter *or* for their country. But in the end, they felt that it would be a wonderful opportunity for the two countries to see each other as more human, and to show that Americans and Soviets were both decent, family-oriented people. Thanks to this decision, Samantha would soon become a household name not only in the small town of Manchester, Maine, but throughout the entire world.

GETTING READY

The Soviet ambassador sent Samantha's family details about the trip. It would last for two weeks, and everything would be paid for by the Soviet government, including the family's $10,000 first class plane tickets. Samantha's visit would include three stops. First, she would see Moscow, the capital of the Soviet Union. Next, she would stay at a children's camp called Artek off the Black Sea. And finally, she would tour the historic Soviet city of Leningrad before returning back to Moscow. Arthur Smith joked that Samantha had no idea what this trip would be like, but that it would definitely be more of an adventure than just going to Grandma's house. Samantha had no trouble keeping busy before the big day. She finished fifth grade, answered some of the letters she'd received in the mail, (her father gave up trying to answer them himself after about 1,000!,) started softball practice, and checked out books from the library in order to learn more about the foreign country that she would soon be visiting. A week before her trip was to begin, Samantha gave an interview from her backyard in which she tried to explain the difference between capitalism and communism. "Say you have a big popcorn popper, like at the movies, and you want to sell popcorn. You can't just sell it on the street in Russia, you probably have to get permission," she concluded. Before leaving on her adventure of a lifetime, Samantha also toured the Maine State House, where she met and shook hands with the

Governor of Maine, and was praised by the House and the Senate for the way in which she had "sparked a glimmer of hope in the coldness of international relations." When it came to communicating with the Soviet Union, they said proudly, Samantha had succeeded where so many diplomats, both older and wiser than she, had failed. Head of the Senate Gerald P. Conley remarked that Samantha was one of the most popular citizens in the state of Maine, and that she received even more attention than government officials such as himself. (He then sent her back to school in time for social studies and study hall.) In spite of all the admiration that Samantha received at home in America, she was still worried that the Soviet children might not like her, or maybe even think she was a spy!

THE TRIP BEGINS

Shortly after her 11th birthday, Samantha's grandmother Nonnie and cousin Tyler arrived to stay at the Smiths' house and take care of the family's pets while they were away. On Thursday, July 7th, 1983, Samantha's trip officially began. She woke up early on that sunny morning and got dressed in a colorful, comfortable outfit consisting of light blue pants, a short-sleeved green and white striped shirt, one of her favorite yellow sweaters, and sneakers. Samantha and her family had gone shopping to pick out special gifts to give her Soviet hosts and some of the new friends she would make in the Soviet Union. These presents, which included t-shirts, buttons, stickers, and more souvenirs from the state of Maine, were packed inside of a picnic basket that was put into the car with the Smiths' suitcases and other luggage. Samantha also brought along a present for Yuri Andropov, but she wanted it to be a surprise. When the press in Montreal asked Samantha, (whom one Canadian journalist referred to as "the fresh-faced girl from small town America,") about this mysterious gift, she refused to tell him what it was and jokingly replied, "You reporters can't keep a secret!" When she reached the Augusta State Airport, Samantha said goodbye to Nonnie and Tyler and to some of the photographers that she recognized, and boarded a small plane headed for Boston. The Smith family then flew from Massachusetts to Canada. On this jet flight, the pilot let Samantha sit next to him in the cockpit and take a photo. When Samantha landed in the Canadian capital of Montreal, so many reporters were shouting Samantha's name and shoving each other to get closer to her that she accidentally bit one of the reporter's microphones! Even the Canadian Mounted Police, famous

for riding on horseback, had trouble guiding the Smiths through the crowd. Samantha once remarked that if reporters would just raise their hands, things would stay way more calm, but be far less exciting. When asked later how she felt about the constant media attention, and what it was like having the press following her every move and hanging on her every word, Samantha relented that it wasn't really their fault for always pestering her, because they were just doing their jobs. One whole day later, on Friday morning, Samantha finally landed in the Soviet Union after a non-stop nine hour flight. Samantha had listened to music and watched movies on the plane in order to help pass the time. When Samantha got off the airplane, she noticed that the airport looked just like the ones in America, and she wasn't sure if she was actually in the Soviet Union or not! But there, in the lobby of the Sheremetyevo Airport, two adult guides and ten Soviet children were waiting to greet Samantha with bouquets of flowers. Samantha could barely see because she was surrounded by so many bright camera lights. She gave a quick interview to members of the press in attendance at the airport, saying, "Zdravstkvuite" (Hello) and "Spasibo" (Thank you) and reminding everyone that the Soviet Union and the United States did not want to start a war. "So

why are we still making all these bombs and pointing them at each other?" she inquired. When reporters asked Samantha what she thought of Moscow, she wondered, "How could I answer that when I just walked off the airplane?" Samantha and her parents were then whisked away from the airport in a black limousine to a very beautiful hotel (normally reserved for important visiting dignitaries) that Samantha thought looked like a palace. It even had a piano inside! Samantha rode up and down the escalators a few times and then joined her parents, who wanted to rest. The cooks sent up a fancy cake and bowls of fruit, but Samantha was too tired to eat any. After playing "Chopsticks" on the piano with her mother, she fell asleep. When she woke up from her nap, Samantha wasn't sure where she was at first. It all seemed like a dream, but then she remembered- she was really in the Soviet Union!

TOURING MOSCOW

For dinner her first night in Moscow, Samantha ate in the hotel's huge dining room, where she reported that "if anybody even looked at the waiters, they would rush over to see what we needed, so I had to be careful not to look anywhere near them." She ordered Chicken Kiev, a chicken breast with hot butter in the center, and had to be shown how to cut it so that the butter wouldn't squirt her in the eye! For the rest of her trip, Samantha ordered Chicken Kiev whenever she saw it on the menu. On Saturday morning, after having some time to rest up, Samantha Smith and her parents were given a personal tour of Moscow. Samantha saw many of the city's government buildings in a very old area called the Kremlin, which was completely surrounded by walls. In fact, the word Kremlin actually means "fortress." Samantha also saw huge palaces (one with chandeliers larger than her living room at home!) and churches decorated with gold and full of beautiful religious paintings. Earlier, Samantha and her family were extremely solemn when Samantha's father set a wreath of red flowers near the "eternal flame," a fire that never went out, at the Tomb of the Unknown Soldier, a popular landmark in Moscow. Reporters noted that Samantha was "pale with emotion" as she paid her respects. She and her family then walked a short distance across a cobblestone road to a mausoleum where Samantha and her parents filed past the body of Lenin, the leader of the Russian Revolution, whose remains were kept in a lit up glass case and surrounded by guards at all times. In Samantha's words, Vladimir Lenin was, to the Soviet people, sort of like America's George Washington- an important and respected historical and political figure. Samantha, who had never seen a dead body before, found Lenin's tomb dark and scary. It gave her the creeps, and she was quite relieved once she got back outside. Samantha liked the bright, open area in Red Square where parades and  other celebrations were held much better! After spending all day with grown-ups acting serious and visiting somber places, Samantha was getting bored and looked forward to having fun and meeting lots of Soviet children closer to her own age the next day at Camp Artek. She was also glad to stop walking, and later revealed, "My feet started hurting because the shoes that looked best on me were too small." To reach Artek, Samantha had to take yet another short airplane ride to a southern part of the Soviet Union known as the Crimea, a hilly area surrounded by the Black Sea near a town called Yalta. Although Samantha once admitted to a reporter that she didn't like camps, Artek turned out to be her favorite part of the trip.

CAMP ARTEK

When her plane landed on the Crimean peninsula where Camp Artek is located, Samantha was greeted by a group of pioneers aged 9-14 bearing flowers and wearing uniforms similar to those worn by Girl Scouts and Boy Scouts in the United States. (Samantha herself had been a Girl Scout and her mother, Jane, had been a scout leader.) For the duration of her stay at Camp Artek, Samantha would wear the same white shirt and navy blue skirt and cap worn by all of the other pioneer children. However, she did not wear their traditional red scarf, which stood  for communism, but instead wore a blue scarf that was given to visitors. Samantha liked her uniform so much that she asked to keep it when she left Artek and was given permission, although normally the pioneers returned their uniforms at the end of camp. Many of the campers also gave Samantha their white chiffon hair bows, which she was very fond of. Samantha admitted she was a bit shy at the idea of meeting so many new children all at once, but the second she got off the plane and her feet touched the ground, they were dragging her onto the Artek minibus. During the drive, the other children kept calling her "Samanta!," because there is no "th" sound in the Russian language. From the moment Samantha arrived at

Camp Artek, the young pioneers went out of their way to welcome and entertain their special American guest. Over 1,000 young pioneers sat in bleachers, chanting Samantha's name over the music of a live band. Samantha learned that all of the children invited to Artek were extremely smart and incredibly talented, but she found them to be very nice, too. A 13-year-old girl named Natasha Kashirina welcomed Samantha to Artek, and she and other teenagers presented her with a round loaf of brown bread that had a small white bowl of salt on top, traditional Russian welcoming gifts. Samantha wasn't sure if she was supposed to eat it or not, but finally did- and thought it was delicious! Natasha and Samantha immediately formed a strong bond, and Natasha became Samantha's best friend and constant companion during her stay at Artek. While her parents checked into a nearby hotel, Samantha chose to bunk in a dormitory with nine other Soviet girls. From the balcony at the end of her dorm room, Samantha could see the beach and smell the sea. Although Natasha spoke English fairly well because her mother taught the language at a school in Leningrad, most of the other girls sharing a room with Samantha

spoke very little English- or none at all. Nevertheless, this language barrier would not stop Samantha and her roommates from becoming fast friends. As the Soviet newspaper *Izvestiya* pointed out, "That she does not know Russian will not prevent her from having a good time. Children are very quick to find a common language." Indeed, the girls were soon teaching Samantha Russian songs and dances, and participating in Samantha's favorite pastime at Artek- swimming! Samantha found the Black Sea much cleaner than the lakes full of "gunk" that she swam in back home. Of course, the sea wasn't really black, but it *was* very salty, which made it easier to float in, and Samantha felt like she  was wearing a lifejacket as she swam. Samantha and Natasha enjoyed diving into the sea to search for pretty seashells and interesting pebbles, and Samantha also spoke fondly during one interview about her joyful experiences with jellyfish! "They have hundreds of tons of jellyfish that don't sting in the Black Sea," she revealed, "and you can have jellyfish fights. They're about the size of your palm, and kind of gooey." During the camp's Neptune Festival, there were

swimming races and a water pageant with floats, and the campers even got to push their counselors into the water! At night, the girls in her bunk would ask Samantha what it was like to

live in the United States, but they rarely talked about peace, the reason that Samantha was in their country to begin with. "It seemed strange even to talk about war when we all got along so well together," Samantha explained. "It didn't really seem necessary because none of them hated America, and none of them ever wanted war." Instead, Samantha answered their questions about clothes and music. At bedtime, the girls in Samantha's dorm talked so much that they were warned to "stop yakking." Once their pioneer leader had turned off the lights, the other girls continued whispering, but Samantha usually felt "pooped out," and was way too tired to stay awake. On her second day at Artek, Samantha went on a motorboat ride with about 200 other campers. For this adventure, Samantha was wearing the summer version of the pioneer uniform, which included a turquoise skirt and matching cap. Samantha and Natasha enjoyed strolling around the deck together and talking, and each pioneer was instructed to write out a favorite wish for the future on a scroll of paper. When the boat was about 45 minutes from shore, Samantha leaned over the rail and tossed an old bottle sealed closed with a cork and wax into the sea. The words "Hopefully, we will have peace for the rest of our lives" were written on a note inside. On cue, the other children took turns throwing messages of peace into the deep blue-green water. It was like the Black Sea had been turned into a giant wishing well! After her cruise, Samantha told reporters at a press conference that she thought Artek would be "like nature camp- in tents and stuff. But it's completely different." On the contrary, Artek was filled with elegant gardens and winding roads leading to the sea. When the press then asked

what she would do if she were a magician, Samantha at first seemed confused by the question, but after a bit of explanation and encouragement from her father, Samantha declared that if she could do magic, she would, "Get rid of all the bombs. Destroy the bombs." On her last day in Artek, hundreds of campers gathered outside and danced together in large circles to disco music, did "the chicken dance," and even formed a conga line- including Samantha's parents! When Samantha had trouble following the steps, Natasha helped show her how. That afternoon while sightseeing in Yalta, Samantha met the wife of Charles Schultz, the artist who created and drew the Peanuts comics. Mrs. Schultz presented Samantha and Natasha with Snoopy badges to wear

on their uniforms. During her last night at camp, Artek gave Samantha a 90-minute farewell ceremony that lasted until dark. There were fireworks, parades, and costume shows. Almost a hundred children dressed up as Misha the Bear, who was a symbol of the

Moscow Olympics in 1980, and Samantha was given a stuffed black bear to take back home to America. She was also handed a piece of charred wood from the bonfire that had been burned to signal the end of camp. Before leaving, Samantha gave a tearful farewell speech, which an interpreter translated into Russian for the Soviet children who were listening at Artek and at home on their television sets. Her father admitted that he had mostly written the speech himself after poor Samantha had become unable to articulate herself

at a welcome dinner the week before. "Let our countries be friends," Samantha began. "My stay at sea camp in Artek has been wonderful, very wonderful. I shall miss my new international friends. But we will remain friends across the sea. Let our countries be friends, too. Someday I hope to return. I love you, Artek," Samantha finished, waving into the stadium. Immediately following these heartfelt words, Samantha and her friends sang a goodbye song. Samantha and Natasha had been given permission to spend the night with Jane and Arthur Smith at the Artek Hotel. At around midnight, the two giggling girls got dressed and snuck over to a dinner party next door that Samantha's parents were attending. Once inside, they happily took some cake and soda. Samantha and Natasha were caught and told that Natasha could go to the airport with the Smith family the following morning if they went back to sleep, so the girls promised to go right to bed. Before leaving for Leningrad, Samantha and her parents visited a "collective farm," where 3,000 people lived and worked and went to school. Samantha, wearing a red and white flowered sundress for the occasion, sampled fruit that she plucked straight off the trees. This particular communal farm performed agricultural experiments, and the result was giant-sized fruit. Samantha was amazed to see raspberries the size of ping pong balls!

VISITING LENINGRAD

On Wednesday, Samantha left Artek and headed back north to Leningrad, the second largest city in the Soviet Union and the home of Natasha, who would be meeting her there. Samantha thought that Leningrad was a beautiful ancient city. Originally named St. Petersburg after Czar Peter, the city was later renamed Leningrad (after Vladimir Lenin) following the Russian Revolution, when Czar Peter was overthrown. Samantha learned that much of Leningrad had been destroyed during World War II. The Smiths visited the burial grounds for half a million

soldiers who had died during the second world war when the city was bombed by Germany for nearly three years. Sad funeral music played as Samantha walked past moss covered graves and left a wreath at the cemetery's large memorial wall, near a sculpture representing the brave soldiers and civilians who refused to surrender to the Nazis and kept the Germans from taking over the city. Samantha then toured another monument, this time a battleship from 1917 named the Aurora. The ship was famous for giving the signal that started the Russian Revolution, and had since been turned into a museum. A young sailor presented Samantha with five red carnations when she stepped on board the ship. Samantha inspected the small radio room where important messages were sent to sea. When she left, the ship's captain gave Samantha a white ceramic polar bear wearing a sailor's handkerchief. On Friday, the limousine that Samantha and her family were using to drive around Leningrad suddenly refused to start. Embarrassed Soviet officials sent over another car, this time a black and silver sedan that looked like an American car from the 1950's, and Samantha was able to continue her tour. She met with more Soviet children at the Pioneer Palace, where she played table hockey. When a child presented her with an embroidered apron, a white crocheted purse, and a paper mache peacock, Samantha exclaimed, "They made them, oh, my gosh!" Samantha confessed that she was jealous of how well many Soviet children could sew. She claimed they made teddy bears that looked as though they came right out of a store! From there, Samantha visited with much younger children at a Soviet "sanatorium," or hospital for sick children. Samantha happily played with a preschool-aged group, holding their hands and running with them in the grass, until it came time to go on a giant slide. It was one of the biggest slides that Samantha had ever seen, and at first, she was afraid to let go of the bar that was keeping her from sliding down. Finally, as spectators encouraged her and cheered her on, Samantha gathered her courage and slowly released her grip on the sides of the slide. She let out a brief shriek on the way down, but in a flash she found herself already back on the ground. That night, Samantha attended a professional ballet performance at the renowned Kirov Theater. The inside was decorated entirely in blue and gold, and Samantha called it the most beautiful place she'd ever seen. Samantha thought the three hour ballet was going to be boring, but it turned out to be "terrific." During the traditional break following the first act of the ballet, a Soviet guide gave Samantha a tour of the backstage area, but it was so dark that Samantha could hardly see. Suddenly, Russian prima ballerina Alla Sizova ran up to Samantha and handed her a pair of toe shoes in which she had just finished dancing. She quickly autographed the ballet slippers before rushing off to prepare for the next part of her performance. Samantha was so excited about trying on the silky pink slippers (which fit perfectly, thanks to her "big feet!") she could barely pay attention to the rest of

the ballet! Because it is located so close to the North Pole, Leningrad has what is called "white nights" in the summertime, and when Samantha and her family left the ballet at 11 p.m., the sun was just going down! Samantha had a hard time sleeping until it actually got dark. On her final day in Leningrad, Samantha and her mother were joined by Natasha and her mother on a boat ride to the summer palace of Czar Peter on the Gulf of Finland. The Czar's palace was famous for its many fountains, including the "trick" fountains whose water suddenly turns on and off. If you stepped on the wrong stone as you walked, you could instantly get soaked. Samantha and Natasha had lots of fun trying to maneuver around the fountains without getting drenched, but they weren't always successful! Samantha warned a nearby reporter to watch out or her camera might get wet. At a tea hosted by the House of Peace and Friendship that same afternoon, a Russian schoolgirl named Tugaleva told Samantha, "War is a tragedy for all mankind. On your return to the United States, I would like you to tell your friends… that Soviet children are for peace." Two brothers also gave Samantha a copy of *Alice in Wonderland* written in Russian for her to read once she had learned their language. When Samantha left the palace, she wrote this message in the guest book: "Peace To All Of Our Kind. Samantha Smith." After lunch, Samantha showed Natasha her autographed toe shoes. At Samantha's request, Natasha, who was a talented ballerina, put on the ballet slippers and demonstrated how she could stand straight up on the tips of her toes! Samantha also tried standing on her toes while holding onto a chair but said that it "hurt like crazy!" Samantha and Natasha then played a duet on a gold-trimmed piano they found on the second floor of the hotel. Samantha knew that Natasha had to go home later that day, and she wished that the two of them could have kept on playing forever. Before leaving, Natasha went with Samantha to the famous Hermitage Museum, which had once been Czar Peter's winter palace but was now the largest museum in the world. In fact, there are so many works of art inside, it would take six years to see them all if you looked at each piece for

just one minute! Samantha and Natasha only had time to look through a few of the many fancy rooms. When the moment came for Natasha and her mother to leave, Samantha and Natasha slipped into the backseat of the limousine for one last chat. When they emerged, the two girls hugged and said goodbye. Samantha invited Natasha to visit her in America, but warned, "Don't make a big story out of it!" to the reporters who were listening. "It's just a thought, a hope," she reminded them, but added, "My parents said it's okay." Unfortunately, the Soviet Union had very strict rules when it came to their citizens travelling to the United States and other countries in the West. Sadly, Samantha would never get the chance to see Natasha again.

RETURNING TO MOSCOW

The Leningrad Friendship Society hosted a dinner party for the Smiths before they returned to Moscow. Since everyone was giving toasts, Samantha decided to give one, too. Using a wine glass full of Pepsi, she toasted the cameraman from Maine who had once fallen down because he had to walk backwards in front of Samantha in order to film her. That night, Samantha and her family rode a midnight "sleeper" train with pull-down beds back to Moscow. After having some tea and walking up and down the aisles passing out pastries to the news people and Soviet officials who were accompanying her, Samantha headed to her compartment for the night. The clickety-clack sound of the moving train tracks helped her fall asleep right away. On Saturday, exactly one week after Samantha had first arrived in the Soviet Union, the Smith family was back in Moscow, but to Samantha, it felt more like months had passed. The Ambassador of Moscow invited Samantha and her family to his home for lunch, where they served a very American meal of hamburgers and french fries! For the next several days, Samantha stayed extremely busy. She toured the subways, which were like underground palaces with chandeliers and very long, very fast, very steep escalators. At the Krylatskoye Olympic Training Center inside of a dome-like stadium, Samantha got to ride a racing bicycle, but since it was way too big for her, the bike had to be adjusted and a cycling specialist rode on either side of her in case of an emergency. She also got gymnastics lessons from Soviet elite gymnasts. Samantha had a great time doing cartwheels on the floor, swinging on the uneven bars, jumping over the vault, and walking on the balance beam. A rhythmic gymnast even taught Samantha how to twirl a long silk ribbon

into pretty shapes. When Samantha attended the Moscow Circus, which is one of the most famous circuses in the entire world, she was given a ride to the arena in a horse-drawn sleigh. Near the front entrance, reporters snapped photos as Samantha enthusiastically pet a real live bear. Once inside and seated, Samantha was handed a bouquet of pink roses and got stuck by a thorn. "Ow!" she exclaimed, temporarily in pain. She explained to her concerned mother what had happened before quickly shaking it off and giving the cameras her signature grin. Ironically, it was Samantha herself who was one of the circus's main attractions that night. A performer drew a sketch of her, and a man seated two rows in front of her shouted, "Hi, Samantha! I'm from California!" At one point, while waiting for an act to begin, Samantha started batting a balloon back and forth with other members of the audience. Samantha's favorite part of the circus was the animals, and when asked which ones she liked the best, Samantha answered, "All of them." From there, Samantha went to an animal theater (similar to a zoo) where she saw a cat playing a miniature piano. At the Moscow Puppet Theater, Samantha got a lesson on how to maneuver the different parts of a puppet to make it move, and after touring a toy museum, she was given a traditional Russian nesting doll called a Matryoshka. Inside of the foot tall, hand-painted wooden doll were six smaller, identical dolls that could be stacked inside of each other. As if her day hadn't been incredible enough, Samantha even got to meet Valentina Tereshkova, the first female astronaut (or, as the Soviets

say, cosmonaut) to go into space back in 1963, where she completed a 70-hour flight orbiting the Earth. Samantha was a little bit embarrassed when they met, because she had accidentally hung up on Tereshkova a week earlier when she answered the phone and heard what she thought was just a kid saying, "I kiss you, Samantha! I kiss you!" Her blue eyes widened in surprise when she learned of her mistake, and realized who she'd really spoken to! "I didn't know it was the first woman in space. Geez!," Samantha exclaimed afterwards. When they met in person, Samantha joked that Tereshkova hugged her to pieces. During their hour-long meeting at the office of the Soviet Women's Committee, Samantha and Tereshkova talked not only about military spending, but also bikes, stars, and horses. Tereshkova showed Samantha a special collection of over 100 dolls from around the world that had been given to her as gifts from foreign visitors. Samantha found Tereshkova to be a very thoughtful and important person, and hoped that she would become the first woman president of the Soviet Union someday. On her next to last day in Moscow, Samantha got a beautiful view of the city from the hills near the state university, in which she could see one of seven "wedding cake" skyscrapers located in the Soviet capital, then briefly toured the monastery where Peter the Great had imprisoned his own sister. Unfortunately, Samantha was unable to see much of the famous Bolshoi Theatre because it was undergoing repairs during the summer months. Still, officials were so proud of what Samantha was trying to accomplish during her Soviet visit that they pinned a commemorative medal onto her jumper, the kind usually only given to the theatre's best performers. Samantha was embarrassed that she had only a small pin from the state of Maine to give them in return. This whirlwind morning was followed by a farewell luncheon hosted in Samantha's honor by the Friendship Society. Samantha wore a traditional Russian folk costume and a high pearl headdress with a pointy top that was made for her by Soviet children. While everyone was eating, Samantha would occasionally sneak off to

play the piano. Waiters and waitresses passed out food, and Samantha had decorated gingerbread cookies for dessert. Samantha wrote that the Soviet people loved children, and she felt quite spoiled that day!

SAYING GOODBYE

On Wednesday, July 20th, the Smith family's last day in Moscow before they would return to the United States, Samantha learned that she was not going to be meeting with Yuri Andropov, as she had been hoping. The 69-year-old Soviet leader was not in the best of health, and also had an important meeting planned with the leader of Hungary. Instead, a Soviet official named Leonid Zamyatin arrived bearing gifts from the Soviet leader, including a decorative silver teapot, a freshly painted, shiny wooden lacquer box with a picture of Red Square on the top, (Samantha laughingly said that she could still smell the drying paint!) and two 100-page photo albums filled with black and white pictures chronicling Samantha's visit. Samantha gave Andropov a present, as well- a book containing all of Mark Twain's speeches, because he liked Mark Twain's stories and as the Soviet leader, he had to make a lot of speeches himself! Samantha wasn't too disappointed that she didn't get to meet Andropov in person. "I feel I did get through to him in a way," she said, adding that she "probably couldn't have said anything to him anyway." She rationalized, "He's a busy man. He's the President of Russia. I'm just a little American girl. I mean, he shouldn't just take time off and cancel a thousand meetings just to see me." Zamyatin helpfully tried to answer himself some of the questions that Samantha had asked Andropov in her letter. By now, Samantha was much less worried about the United States and the Soviet

Union getting into a war. At a press conference held in Moscow the following morning shortly before the Smiths headed home, Samantha said that people who have been to the Soviet Union know that the Soviets don't want war, they just want peace. When asked why some Americans are afraid of Soviets or have the wrong idea about them, Samantha replied, "Well, for one thing, they probably never met a Soviet person, and those people have never been to Russia." Samantha insisted that it wasn't fair for people to judge the Soviets if they hadn't been to Russia and seen what it's really like. On a lighter note, Samantha proudly announced that she now

knew 23 Russian words, and recited a few of these foreign phrases into her microphone at the request of a journalist in the audience. Upon leaving the conference room, Samantha cheerfully told reporters, "In three days, I'll see you in America!" She then marveled at the many wrapped parcels awaiting her outside. "Look at all this stuff!" she exclaimed. She struggled to carry the heavy box holding the Samovar teapot into a waiting car, but then handed it over to her father, joking, "If you hold it for awhile, it gains weight!" While the grown-ups tried to figure out how to fit all of Samantha's presents into the

vehicle, Samantha climbed into the backseat and waved out the window at the lines of well-wishers standing on the sidewalk and surrounding her car. Samantha loaded film into her Polaroid instant camera as she prepared to leave, taking a few final photos of her Soviet admirers. Samantha was soon boarding a plane bound for Maine, but since there are no non-stop flights from the Soviet Union to the United States, Samantha had her first layover in Montreal, where the family planned to get a good night's sleep before their second plane ride, which would stop in Boston. The first thing a very tired Samantha did when landing at the airport was to drink an entire Coke really fast! Samantha, an avid softball player and baseball fan, had hoped to see the Montreal Expos play ball against the Cincinnati Reds that night during her stopover in Canada. She had asked for free tickets, but the club thought that the media coverage of Samantha might disrupt the paying ticketholders attending the game. Samantha's father told Canadian reporters he was eager to get home, get himself reoriented to everyday life, and relax, but that his daughter had other plans. Samantha announced that if her best friend Lynn wasn't waiting for her at the airport when she got back to Maine, she was going to "go home and call her up and tell her to come see me." Samantha considered her trip a success, but was still glad to see it coming to an end. "I had a lot of fun, but I'm homesick," she admitted. Arthur Smith, who had suffered a second heart attack shortly before his daughter wrote her life-changing letter, applauded Samantha for successfully handling two full weeks of twelve-hour days, and displaying enthusiasm and eagerness with everyone she met, everywhere she went. He felt that "very few people could have done what she did." Jane Smith agreed, declaring, "She was the perfect age for all this. She had no idea of the impact... It was like she was taking an exciting field trip. A couple more years down the road and she would have been too self-conscious."

After witnessing life up-close in the Soviet Union, Samantha insisted that the Soviets were a peace loving people "very much like us." She later relented, "It's a lot stricter there, but that's nothing to accuse them of. It's just a different way of living. It doesn't hurt us." Many members of the press and the United States government felt that Samantha had been used by the Soviet Union as a propaganda tool, and believed that in order to make their country and their people look good, they showed Samantha and other Americans only the best parts of their communist nation. "Some people ask," Samantha once said, "'Well, don't you think they set it all up?' Well, *of course* they did," she exclaimed. "I mean, what are they going to do, show me the grossest parts of all, or just let me wander around on my own? Of *course* not!" she repeated. "If I had a new friend come over to my house I wouldn't take them down in the basement," she added as a comparison. "The press kept saying, 'You only saw what they wanted you to see,'" remarked her father Arthur. "Well, the truth is, we saw exactly what we asked to see." He also pointed out that the Soviet government took a big risk inviting a 10-year-old to their county along with a slew of news media, because they had no idea of what her reaction would be. Instead of enjoying herself, Samantha could just as easily have said, "I hate this, I want to go home!" when in front of the cameras. Yet, the Soviets put their faith in Samantha and placed high hopes on her visit. Samantha admitted, "Well, I think they were using me, but it was propaganda for peace… to get me over there so I could see what it was like, and come back and tell people how nice it was." Arthur Smith believed that the Soviets wanted Americans to see them as real people with families and dreams for their children, and not the "evil empire" that they were often portrayed as in the United States.

COMING HOME

Meanwhile, back in Manchester, Maine, a big homecoming was being prepared for little Samantha Smith. While her grandmother baked cookies, her cousin decorated the Smith's home with red, white, and blue streamers and a giant "Welcome Home" banner that hung from the roof. Signs on local storefronts that normally displayed the price of milk or eggs had changed to "Congratulations, Samantha Smith." On Friday, Samantha landed at the Augusta State Airport, and hundreds of people were there to greet her, cheering and holding signs and balloons and waving American flags. A red carpet had been rolled out for Samantha to walk on, but the second her feet hit the ground, she ran straight into her grandmother's arms for a giant hug. "I'm happy to be getting home to regular things," said Samantha, adding that while the Soviet Union was a nice place to visit, "I'd rather live in my hometown."  Although a chauffeur-driven, black and maroon Rolls Royce limousine awaited her, it took a station wagon to carry the twenty-something pieces of Samantha's luggage weighing over 200 pounds. (She had started her trip with only seven suitcases!) One Soviet reporter even claimed that Samantha had been given teddy bears in five different colors. Cameras rolled as Samantha tried, unsuccessfully, to squeeze a huge balloon bouquet into the vehicle with her, but it just wouldn't fit. "Everywhere we went we got gifts," Samantha's mother explained. Samantha's father decreed, "No more letter-writing for awhile, except for thank you notes." When she finally reached the front doorstep of the Smith's white, cape cod style house in Maine, an overjoyed Samantha clicked the heels of her sneakers together three times and repeated, "There's no place like home! There's no place like home!" Once inside, she immediately began to unpack and put

on a pair of sandals with spiked heels given to her by a fellow Artek pioneer. Samantha also began admiring some of her other presents, including a tea set, but she had very little time to get settled in. As the guest of honor at the Manchester Day Parade the following day, people lined the streets and waited patiently in order to catch a glimpse of their hometown hero, who was seated in between her parents as she drove past in a light blue convertible, holding roses with one arm, and waving happily or throwing candy into the crowd with the other. Some of her softball teammates rode in the back of a pickup truck a few cars behind Samantha, occasionally shouting out, "Hi, Sam!" At the end of her mile-long route, Samantha stepped onto a platform set up on the lawn of her elementary school in front of hundreds of fellow Manchester residents. Samantha, wearing a bright green shirt, white print skirt, and knee socks, stood casually next to the Governor, confessing to him that she had woken up at 3 a.m. due to the time change. When Manchester officials handed her an enormous, sparkly "Key to the City," Samantha exclaimed, "I must be dreaming!" When asked to give a speech, Samantha giggled and said bashfully, "Thanks an awful lot! I'm awful glad to be home." Overwhelmed, Samantha covered her face for a moment after she sat down. Several of Samantha's friends noticed that she was wiggling her toes. They knew this was something that Samantha often did when she was nervous.

BACK IN THE NEWS

After returning to America, Samantha continued to make headlines. On her first day of school and only two months since her trip to Russia, the Soviet Union destroyed a Korean jetliner, shooting it out of the sky and killing 260 people. News crews immediately scrambled to interview Samantha and get her reaction, even going inside of her classroom and taking a picture of the sixth grader sitting at her desk. Samantha declared that this action taken by the Soviets

was "a really horrible thing to do," but claimed that she still trusted them, and encouraged talking about the incident. Samantha also made repeat television appearances. During her second Johnny Carson interview, Samantha sat very still and stiff in her chair. Her friends had teased her for wiggling around in her seat and swinging her dangling legs like a little kid during her first *Tonight Show* interview, when her feet didn't reach the floor. Then, in order to wrap up her whole experience, Samantha and her father co-wrote a book about her trip entitled *Journey to the Soviet Union*. Otherwise, Samantha's life more or less returned to normal (although she would still get recognized at places like the grocery store, which she thought was "neat.") She played on her softball league, ate popsicles, listened to rock music, and took care of her pets (which now included a puppy and a terrarium full of twenty mice!) She remained pen pals with Natasha Kashirina, and hoped that one day they would meet again in person. Samantha's parents also treated her the same way they always had. Even in junior high, Samantha's bedtime was at 8:30 p.m., and her father had to approve the outfits that she wore to public functions. Even after all of the attention she'd received, a classmate of Samantha's told reporters, "She didn't act like she was different from us, she acted the same as  everyone else did." Samantha's school advisor agreed. "She was such a normal kid in light of all that fame and fortune," he said. Still, Samantha had encountered some problems upon her return to school. A few of her fellow students teased her and called her a communist. Samantha had also fallen behind in her homework and some of her subjects. One teacher told Samantha that her on-set tutor had shown her the wrong way to do an assignment, and then ripped up her paper in front of the whole class, bringing Samantha to tears. But such incidents were few and far between, and Samantha's life soon settled back into her old routine. Five months after her legendary trip to the Soviet Union, however, all that changed when Samantha left the country once again.

TRAVELING TO JAPAN

The year 1983 had already been a very busy one for Samantha Smith when she was unexpectedly invited to attend the Children's International Symposium for the 21st Century in Kobe, Japan- an event that focused on the future and the use of technology. During her ten day trip, which took place over the Christmas holiday, Samantha met the Japanese prime minister, observed the printing press at a Japanese newspaper, visited ancient Japanese temples, posed for a photo in front of a giant robot made of ice, drank from three waterfalls that claimed to  bring good health, and drew a dipper full of water from a "magical" wishing well. The Japanese people referred to Samantha as "The Angel of Peace," and she was often recognized on the streets while she was sightseeing. Japanese housewives would even hand Samantha their handkerchiefs to sign! On December 25th, Samantha and her mother ate Chinese food for their Christmas dinner. The next day, Samantha met with a group of Japanese schoolchildren who had won a newspaper contest in which they were instructed to write a composition on "What the Year 2001 Means to Me." Samantha then gave her own speech at the symposium, which ended up being less about science and more about peace. After suggesting

that computers could someday be used to locate food and give it to people who didn't have any, she proposed that the United States and the Soviet Union start a granddaughter exchange program for two weeks every year, similar to the trip that she herself had taken that summer. Her reasoning was that a world leader "wouldn't want to send a bomb to a country his granddaughter was visiting." Then, she explained, these children could "come back and tell people what the place was like, and hopefully, usually, most of the news would be, 'these other people are nice people.'" She also made a wish that by the 21st century, "We will be able to look around and find only friends. When I think of the year 2001, I can picture people who don't look the same as me being my very good friends." Samantha stated her personal belief that everyone could be friends, and anyone could get along if they just tried hard enough.

THE REPORTER

In January of 1984, the Disney Channel, which was impressed by Samantha's composure on television and her interest in world politics at such a young age, offered Samantha the opportunity to interview Democratic presidential candidates about the upcoming election, which would be filmed for a tv special called *Samantha Smith Goes to Washington*. This time around, Samantha would be the one asking the questions instead of answering them! Before the interviewing began, Samantha visited elementary school classrooms in Boston and Washington to collect the questions that she would ask the presidential hopefuls, so that her interviews would reflect what children, and not just adults, wanted to know about the candidates. She also gathered questions from the thousands of letters that she had received from young people, so in a way, "she was acting as a representative of children from around the world." Wearing professional attire that included a tweed jacket and skirt, Samantha asked the candidates questions that were both tough and fun. For instance, she learned the candidates' opinions on the federal budget *and* their favorite movies. Samantha shared personal information about herself with the candidates, as well. She admitted that she'd gotten into trouble for sliding down the stairs on a mattress, and once ran away from home- for 15 minutes. She also told a reporter during this time that for her 12th birthday, she would like world peace or a kitten. One day, Samantha found out that the only way she could interview Senator Alan Cranston was to immediately board a plane for California, which she did. Samantha arrived from the East Coast wearing heavy winter clothing, and felt extremely overdressed for the 80 degree weather. Samantha took this job very seriously. She stayed up so late every night writing questions and researching candidates that she didn't even have time to watch television. "It was really tiring," she later recalled. Nevertheless, Samantha enjoyed this experience so much that she was starting to consider a career in journalism when she grew up. The highlight of this job for Samantha, however, was not meeting the possible future president of the United States, but actor Ricky Schroeder, a major teen idol at the time! Unfortunately, one person Samantha would never get to meet was Yuri Andropov, whose death was reported on February 10, 1984, shortly after Samantha returned home  from her Disney reporting job. Samantha received a telephone call that morning at 6 a.m. Although she was sick in bed with the flu, Samantha still went downstairs and gave a statement to the press over the phone. "I was shocked. I never almost met someone who ended up dying!" she exclaimed.

THE TV STAR

In July of 1984, exactly one year after her historic trip, Samantha was still working on answering the 2,000-3,000 letters she had received in the mail, mostly from Soviet children praising her courage, which her father had collected and stacked neatly in boxes. "I never thought it would result in all this," Samantha admitted. "I hope it's done some good for our country. Otherwise, it's been a lot of fun travelling. I even lost my airsickness!" she revealed. Samantha also didn't mind when complete strangers would approach her in places like the grocery store and say, "Hi, Samantha." She thought it was "neat." That fall, knowing how

popular Samantha Smith still was with young people across the country, Samantha was invited to appear on an episode of the CBS television show *Charles in Charge*. Samantha had a bit part as one of the girls invited to a slumber party being chaperoned by the family babysitter, a college student named Charles. Samantha only spoke a few lines in the episode, but she appeared in many scenes and had a great time. Afterwards, Samantha told *Barbie* magazine that in the future, she would like to travel more and maybe act on tv again. Later that same year, both of these dreams came true when Samantha received her biggest invitation yet- the chance to audition for a regular part in an ABC television series! The show's producers had seen Samantha, now 12, being interviewed on *The Tonight Show,* and thought she might be just the young actress they'd been looking for. Samantha

jumped at the opportunity, although at first she was worried about going away because her dog had just had puppies. But after getting her parents' approval, Samantha flew to California to try out for the role of Elizabeth Culver on a new detective series named *Lime Street*. Unfortunately, after her audition, which took place in front of twenty of the network's top executives, Samantha was near tears. "I thought I did really terrible," she remembered, but then the show's writer came over and told her she had the part. "When I found out I was screaming!" she exclaimed. It turned out Samantha had no reason to worry. Everyone thought she was a natural. The seventh grader had come a long way from the little girl who was too shy to audition for the fifth grade play! Although Samantha was super happy, she knew this would mean missing even more things back home. Already, she had been unable to attend her school's

Christmas dance and her best friend's birthday party. Samantha accepted the fact that she would not be going back to school in the fall, and admitted, "I know that I'll miss seeing my friends during those five minute breaks between classes. That's sad. I liked sports in school, but I still can go to the beach," she consoled herself. During a news report, Samantha stood in the snow wearing a heavy coat with the cold turning her cheeks pink and laughed, "It's a lot warmer there!"

LIME STREET

During the summer after seventh grade, Samantha filmed the first four episodes of *Lime Street* in Virginia. For her part, only child Samantha got to have an on-screen little sister, ride horses, and even drive a jeep! Although Samantha had never taken a single acting lesson, the crew commented on how dedicated, prepared, and talented the young actress was. Hoping the show would become a success, Samantha's parents were already making plans to relocate from rural Maine to the Los Angeles area in order to accommodate their daughter's busy filming schedule, even putting a deposit on an apartment near Columbia Studios. Some of Samantha's friends back home thought she was crazy for moving all the way across the country to become a "star." Meanwhile, Samantha had become close friends with Courtney and Natasha Wagner, the daughters of Robert Wagner, the well-known actor who played her father on the show. The girls were near Samantha's age, and their huge closets full of designer clothing got Samantha, who in the past had dressed somewhat like a tomboy in her Izod shirts and Calvin Klein jeans, more interested in fashion. "When she first became famous, she never had a dress on," Samantha's mother revealed. "When she met the governor, she didn't even have a pair of dress shoes. I thought she couldn't go in sneakers to meet the governor, so I bought her her first pair of dress ups." Samantha also changed her hairstyle before production on *Lime Street* began. After getting permission from both her mother and the show's producers, Samantha cut her long, straight hair into a short pageboy style that ended just above her shoulders, and added bangs. Samantha liked her new look much better than the "horrible" ponytail she wore in the Soviet Union. By the time the *Lime Street* pilot was picked up as a weekly television series and she began taping more episodes of the show, Samantha had gotten her first perm. Samantha's father, who had given up his teaching position to travel with his daughter, accompanied Samantha on her acting jobs. Mr. Smith joked that he was now just a "baggage carrier," because instead of working he was always carrying around luggage for his famous daughter. The fifth episode of *Lime Street* was filmed on location in London. The episode had been going well, and Samantha had completed most of her scenes. The majority of the  adult cast and crew stayed behind in England while Samantha and her father headed home for a break. Samantha hoped the show would go on for many years, but after receiving a camera for Christmas, she commented, "If an acting career doesn't follow me, I'll probably become a freelance photographer." Cleary, Samantha had many interests and ideas when it came to her future. In July of 1985, she told the television program *Entertainment Tonight* that if she hadn't written to Andropov and become an actress, she might have ended up as a hair stylist or a makeup artist!

THE CRASH

On August 25th, 1985, Samantha's mother awaited her family's return from London at the Augusta State Airport near Manchester, which Samantha had been using quite frequently since her trip to the Soviet Union two years before. Earlier, Samantha and her father had left Boston on a small commuter plane headed for Maine, and Jane was expecting their arrival at any moment. Tragically, Samantha's plane had taken a sudden detour half a mile from the airport. It was a rainy evening with heavy fog and little visibility, and the airplane's crew was fairly new and unfamiliar with the travel route. Whatever the reason, as the plane approached the airport at approximately 10:20 p.m., it was obvious that something was terribly wrong. Residents reported seeing the aircraft flying way too low and shearing the tops off of trees. Some locals heard the plane fly over their homes and mistook the sound for the rumbling of thunder. Unable to gain enough altitude to reach the airport or to land properly, the plane had skidded about 100 feet on the ground before going over an embankment and crashing in a wooded area. The plane exploded on impact and burst into flames, killing all eight passengers on board- including Arthur and Samantha Smith. It wasn't until her husband and daughter's plane was an hour late that Jane Smith began to sense that something might be wrong. The man behind the counter at the airport kept walking in and out of his office, and looked very distressed. Finally, he approached

Mrs. Smith and said, "I'm sorry, it's down." Jane was momentarily puzzled before he explained that the plane she was waiting for had crashed. Jane Smith didn't know what to do. She had no idea if Samantha and Arthur were dead or alive, or whether she should stay at the airport or go to the crash site. In the end, she used a taxi driver's phone to call a neighbor, and they headed

to the scene of the accident, which was blocked off by emergency crews to keep the press and onlookers away. Once the police learned of her identity, Mrs. Smith and her friend were allowed to walk through the crowd. The two women stood at the top of a hill, looking down into a ravine at the wreckage that was left of the plane, which was covered in the white foam that firefighters had used to put out the flames. It didn't appear that there were any survivors, and Jane Smith cried the whole time. Mrs. Smith and her neighbor then drove back home to Manchester, where her mother-in-law Theresa Smith was awaiting the arrival of her beloved son and granddaughter. Jane tried to gently break the news that Samantha and Arthur would never be coming home. Likewise, Raymond Austin, the director of

Lime Street, rushed to inform the cast and crew of the tragedy before it was made public. Samantha's on-screen father, Robert Wagner, was devastated. Samantha had described Wagner as being like a "second father" to her, and she was wearing a gold bracelet that had been a gift from him when she was killed. It was simply inscribed, "To Samantha, With Love. R.J." Austin remembered, "It was a terrible shock. When we finished shooting…and Samantha was ready to leave with her father, she had a script…that she got us all to sign. That night, when they showed the newsreel footage of the crash site, the camera panned over the wreckage and came to settle on the script for *Lime Street* with all of our signatures on it." This upset actor Robert Wagner greatly. "The last time I saw Samantha," he remembered, "she came to me with a copy of the script and asked me to sign it. I inscribed the script, 'You know I love you,' and I did." In return, the day before she died Samantha secretly

left Wagner a copy of her book *Journey to the Soviet Union* with the inscription, "R.J., you know I love *you!*" written inside. Wagner also had the heartbreaking task of answering questions about the accident from his daughters, who had befriended Samantha and had already suffered an almost unbearable tragedy only five years earlier when their mother, actress Natalie Wood, had drowned at sea in a boating accident. Like Samantha, Natalie had been a child star and had appeared in the classic Christmas movie *A Miracle on 34th Street* when she was just eight years old. Hopefully, the fact that Samantha and her father had died in each other's arms came as a comfort to the sisters. When *Lime Street* producer Harry Thomason heard the words "little Samantha Smith" on the radio as he was packing for a flight, he at first thought the channel was going to promote their new tv show. When the announcer instead said that Samantha had been killed in a plane crash, he dropped to his knees on the hotel floor. In a statement released after her daughter's death, Jane Smith proclaimed,

"Samantha could not accept man's inhumanity to man. I hope they'll remember her as a lively, optimistic girl who's caused them to do some more thinking about…how we get along with each other in this world." Before leaving London, Samantha sent a "punk rock" postcard to Jessica Jones, a 13-year-old friend and classmate, which Jessica read aloud on television: "Told you I'd write. We went shopping today. I got a lot of stuff, but I'm not telling what til I get home. Miss you. Love, Samantha." Jessica was choking back tears by the time she finished reading the card, which hadn't arrived in the mail until shortly after she'd learned of Samantha's death.

GOODBYE, SAMANTHA

A funeral for Samantha Smith and her father Arthur was held at St. Mary's Roman Catholic Church in Augusta, Maine on Wednesday, August 29th, 1985. Over 800 people crammed the seats and aisles, with hundreds more standing outside listening over a loudspeaker and watching the service on a small television set in the middle of the church's lawn. Samantha's tv father Robert Wagner escorted Jane Smith into the church. The alter was decorated with a bouquet of red and white carnations and white doves sent by the Soviet Embassy, along with floral arrangements from Wagner and Samantha's eighth grade class at Hodgdon Middle School. Samantha was eulogized by Peter Misner, who was not only a minister, but also the Smith's next door neighbor. A children's choir sang "We are the World," and a piano organist played the poignant song "Let There Be Peace on Earth." Soviet Ambassador Vladimir Kulagin, in attendance at the request of new Soviet leader Mikhail Gorbachev, declared, "Samantha shone like a brilliant beam of sunshine at a time when relations between our two countries were clouded."

Meanwhile, a separate memorial service with many of the *Lime Street* cast and crew members was held in Switzerland, where filming was still in production. Inside a small chapel, Samantha was given a "last round of applause," which is a well-known custom that is carried out when an actor dies. On September 21, 1985, the 90-minute *Lime Street* pilot movie aired on

ABC, followed by the four episodes in which Samantha appeared. The show then went on hiatus, and although three additional episodes were filmed after Samantha's death, the series was cancelled. Nobody knew how to deal with the loss of Samantha, and the show would never be the same if Samantha's character was recast or simply disappeared from the series. Finishing the last episode that Samantha appeared in required writing her out of certain scenes that she had not yet filmed, which was difficult on the other actors. Pretending that Samantha's character was in the shower or calling upstairs to her when she wasn't even there gave some of the crew members chills. Without Samantha, the soul of the show was gone. Every *Lime Street* episode ended with a tribute to Samantha which read, "This series is dedicated to Samantha

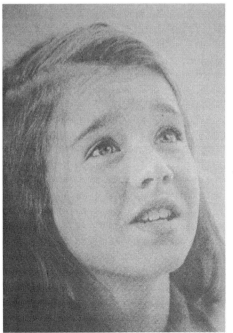

Smith and her dream of peace in the world." The people of the Soviet Union were equally shocked and saddened by Samantha's death. It was Yuri Andropov's successor Gorbachev who had the sorrowful job of informing his country that, "Samantha Smith is no more." The Soviet news program *Today in the World* commented, "It is difficult to believe that the voice of this wonderful American girl will not sound again."

REMEMBERING SAMANTHA

Little Samantha Smith had touched the lives and the hearts of the Soviets in a big way. Following her tragic and unexpected death, the Soviet Union named a priceless diamond and a cultivated flower in her honor. An asteroid discovered between Mars and Jupiter was named 3147 Samantha, and an unnamed Soviet mountain peak is now known as St. Samantha. In 1986, a street in Camp Artek was renamed "Samantha Smith Alley." The Soviet Union also issued a postage stamp which features Samantha's smiling face.

In the United States, a life-sized bronze statue of Samantha holding a dove, the symbol for peace, and standing with a bear at her feet, symbolizing both the state of Maine and the Soviet Union, is located in the Maine state capital of Augusta. The people of Maine spent over a year planning and fundraising the $25,000 that was needed in order to make this special tribute to Samantha become a reality. Much of the money came from schoolchildren and local Maine businesses. At

her mother's request, the sculptor designed Samantha wearing jeans, Nike sneakers, and an imitation Izod t-shirt. (The kind she always bought at Sears.) The plaque affixed to the statue calls Samantha a "young ambassador of goodwill." Schools in Sammamish, Washington and Jamaica, New York now bear the name of Samantha Smith Elementary. The "Samantha Smith Collection" is on permanent display at the Maine State Museum, and features many fascinating artifacts from Samantha's trip that were donated by her mother Jane. In October of 1985, Jane Smith also established the Samantha Smith Foundation to educate young people about peace and encourage friendship between children all over the world. In 1986, Jane and a group of Samantha's classmates returned to the Soviet Union and retraced the steps that Samantha had taken during her historic journey two years before. One of Samantha's classmates remarked, "I was impressed by how well they remembered Samantha and how much they loved her. There were

pictures of her everywhere and a ship that they named after her." The twenty students also got to attend the first Goodwill Games in Moscow, a friendly international sports competition which was dedicated to Samantha, and even met Samantha's Soviet best friend from Camp Artek, Natasha Kashirina. (She, like Samantha, had also cut her long hair short!) Natasha, who today is an elementary school teacher in Los Angeles, shares the story of Samantha with her students every year. She fondly remembers the apprehension felt by many of the Artek campers as they nervously waited to meet Samantha for the first time. Most of them had never met an American girl before, let alone such an important visitor, and had no idea what to expect. When a smiling Samantha came off the plane, one camper sighed with relief, and exclaimed, "She looks just like any girl I know!" Samantha kept in touch with Natasha after her trip, sending her letters and exchanging little presents with her dear Soviet friend. She hoped to one day return to the Soviet Union and see Natasha again, but her busy schedule had made such a visit impossible. As for Jane, after returning from the Soviet Union for the second time in two years, she continued her negotiations with NBC to film a tv movie about Samantha's life, which was to be written and produced by Robert Wagner. For this reason, Mrs. Smith kept Samantha's room exactly as it had been when she died, down to the deflated Snoopy balloon hanging on her wall, so that the creators of the movie would know exactly how it looked. This would help give them a better idea of who the "real" Samantha was- when at home and away from the cameras. In the end, the movie, which was to be called *The Samantha Smith Story*, was never made, because the network decided that there wasn't enough "conflict" in Samantha's inspiring story. Jane dismantled Samantha's room, refusing to let it turn into a shrine to the daughter she had lost. "I didn't want to be the kind of mother who lived in a museum," she explained. "A scriptwriter asked me to leave the room as it was until he could see it, and I did. After that I took pictures of it, so I could remember how it looked." Mrs. Smith donated many of Samantha's mementos from her Soviet trip to the Maine State Library, where they are safely displayed behind a glass case. In the end, Samantha's mother decided to stay in the same familiar town and cozy house that she had once shared with her husband and daughter, although she redecorated and made renovations to the home. Samantha's mother has tried to stay strong and make positive changes come from the death of her husband and only child. She once quoted Samantha's own words: "It's hard to believe how lucky I've been and how much my life was changed by writing that letter. The world seems not so complicated… And the people of the world seem more like people in my own neighborhood. I think they are more like me that I ever realized. I guess that's the most important change inside me. Sometimes I still worry that the next day will be the last day of the Earth. But with more people thinking about the problems of the world, I hope that someday soon we will find the way to world peace. Maybe someone will show us the way." Little did Samantha realize that she was describing herself.

Afterward

I would like to thank Lena and Emir of the Samantha Smith Foundation website (www.samanthasmith.info) for keeping Samantha's memory and dream alive, and for providing such an outstanding resource for information on Samantha Smith.

I would also like to thank the late Todd Wildrick for donating *Lime Street* footage, and Jon Merrill for sharing wonderful videos of Samantha that I was able to share with the entire world and pass on to the Samantha Smith Foundation's Youtube page.

Last but not least, I would like to thank Jane Smith for all of the work she has continued to do on her daughter's behalf.

BIBLIOGRAPHY

Allen, Mel. "Life After Samantha Smith: YANKEE Classic." (2018, February 9). Retrieved from https://newengland.com/today/living/profiles/samantha-smith/

"Animals Make Samantha Laugh." (1983, July 19). *Deseret News*.

De Paul, Tony. "More Than 1000 Mourn Samantha." (1985, August 29). *Bangor Daily News*, p.1.

"First Class Tour Continues for Samantha in Leningrad." (1983, July 15). *Sarasota Herald-Tribune*.

Galicich, Anne. *Samantha Smith: A Journey for Peace*. Minneapolis: Dillon Press, Inc., 1987.

Germani, Clara. "Samantha: An 11 Year Old and World Politics." *The Christian Science Monitor News Service*.

"Girl Brings Presents for Yuri Andropov." (1983, July 8). *The Tuscaloosa News*.

"Girl Launches Message of Peace in Black Sea." (1983, July 11). *The Spokesman Review*.

"Girl Meets First Woman in Space." (1983, July 18). *Spokesman Review*.

"Governor Praises Girl at Hometown Parade." (1983, July 24). *Sarasota Herald-Tribune*, p. 6B.

Hacker, Kathy. "Samantha Smith: Life After the Letter." (1984). *The Philadelphia Enquirer*. Retrieved from: www.samanthasmith.info

Hale, John. "Samantha's Classmates Home." (1986, July 10). *Bangor Daily News*, pp. 1-2.

"In Moscow, Samantha Likes Circus Animals Best." (1983, July 18). *The Montreal Gazette*.

Kany, Howard L. "Samantha Smith Interviews Presidential Candidates." (1984, February 18). *Lewiston Journal*.

Kashirina, Natasha. "Natasha Kashirina Remembers." (2015). Retrieved from http://www.samanthasmith.info/index.php/2-uncategorised/140-natasha-kashirina-remembers

Kliff, Barry. "Littlest Diplomat Takes Peace Plea to Moscow." (1983, July 8). *The Montreal Gazette*.

"Maine Family Greeted." (1983, July 10). *The Victoria Advocate*, p. 3A.

"1,000 Jam Church in Girl's Memory." (1985, August 29). *The New York Times*.

The Phil Donahue Show. Phil Donahue interviews Samantha Smith. (1983, August 16). Video. CBS television.

"A Plane Crash Ends the Bright, Brief Passage of Samantha Smith, America's Littlest Ambassador." (1985, September 9). *People Magazine*, pp. 34-36.

"Pravda Prints Maine Letter, Samantha Waiting for Reply." (1983, April 12). *Bangor Daily News*, pp. 1,3.

"Samantha: 'There's No Place Like Home' as 2-Week Trip Ends." (1983, July 23). *Miami News*.

"Samantha Ends Visit to Russia." (1983, July 21). *The Bulletin*.

"Samantha Gets Medal, Gives Pin to Officials at Theatre." (1983, July 19). *Gadsden Times*.

"Samantha Gets Stuffed Bear." (1983, July 13). *The Palm Beach Post*.

"Samantha Hangs Up On Cosmonaut." (1983, July 15). *Bangor Daily News*.

"Samantha Heads for Moscow." (1983, July 8). *Bangor Daily News*.

"Samantha Proposes Exchange of Granddaughters at Conference." (1983, December 27). *Lewiston Daily Sun*.

"Samantha Receives Slippers from Ballerina." (1983, July 16). *The Telegraph*.

"Samantha Smith Dies in a Plane Crash." *ABC News with Stone Phillips*. Video. Retrieved from https://www.youtube.com/watch?v=SoF9yYMsf-Y

"Samantha Smith Plans Letter to President Reagan." (1983, May 11). *Bangor Daily News*.

"Samantha Tosses Bottle with Message of Peace." (1983, July 11). *Bangor Daily News*, p. 1.

"Samantha Tours Japanese Cities." (1983, December 21). *Spokane Chronicle*.

"Samantha Tours Leningrad." (1983, July 14). *The Telegraph*.

Smale, Alison. "Samantha Ends Soviet Union Tour." (1983, July 20). *The Times News*.

Smith, Samantha. *Journey to the Soviet Union*. Boston: Little, Brown, & Company, 1985.

Snauffer, Douglas. *The Show Must Go On: How the Deaths of Lead Actors Have Affected Television Series*. Jefferson: McFarland Company, Inc., 2008. pp. 138-154.

"Star Wars- The Battle of the Titans." Video. Retrieved from https://www.youtube.com/watch?v=X6vODrvtpfE

"Soviet Greets US Girl." (1983, July 9). *The Victoria Advocate*.

"Soviet Trip Doesn't Turn Samantha from Softball." (1984, July 2). *Toledo Blade*.

The Tonight Show. Johnny Carson interviews Samantha Smith. (1983, July 28). Video. NBC television.

Venezia, Joyce. "Samantha Smith Reacts to Jet Hit." (1983, September 7). *Beaver County Times*.

Warner, Gale and Michael Schuman. *Citizen Diplomats: Pathfinders in Soviet-American Relations- and How You Can Join Them*. New York: The Continuum Publishing Co., 1987. pp. 281-303.

Weible, Jack, "Manchester Girl's Letter to Andropov Published." (1983, April 12). *Kennebec Journal*, p. 1.

Whittaker, Stephanie. "Nice Visit, but Samantha Says She'd Rather Live in Own Country." (1983, July 22). *Montreal Gazette*.

Made in the USA
Middletown, DE
08 February 2023